Towards a Sustainable World

3 Paradigm Shifts To Achieve

2019

Vienna, Austria

In preparing this book for publication, we reached out to a number of the world's foremost thought leaders to gain their comments and feedback about this important book. The responses we received will be valuable to readers in framing their own thoughts about this book, and how they will implement these paradigm shifts in their own personal and professional lives. Please see the Epilogue at the back of the book for extensive and thoughtful testimonials from Marc Dubrulle, Ex officio Member of the Club of Rome, President emeritus, The Club of Rome EU-Chapter; and Father Simon Pierre, Benedictine Monk and lifelong friend of Bernard Lietaer.

Praise for *Toward a Sustainable World*

Our planet is in crisis. More and more people are aware of the harm we are inflicting as we destroy and pollute the natural world whilst at the same time our population grows. We have brought the climate crisis upon ourselves. There is increasing awareness of this, but most people do not take action – they feel helpless. Bernard Lietaer's book provides guidance. Suggests ways we can seek to move forward in greater harmony with nature. We must seek to live more sustainably and remember that each one of us can make a difference – every day.

Jane Goodall, PhD, DBE
Founder, The Jane Goodall Institute & UN Messenger of Peace

Two decades ago, Peter Drucker emphasized: "Change in society has a deeper impact on companies than change in management." Bernard Lietaer's book is a perfect illustration of this paradigm shift illustrated by the sustainability challenge. Leaders need a more holistic approach to the world and to walk the talk. Managers can better rationalize how companies operate by reaching a higher level of efficiency and resilience. People should be aware of the global impact of their lifestyle on the environment. A world of sustainability is one of a different mindset, where information and attitudes are valued differently, and hopefully better. It is a key message in this remarkable book.

Stephane Garelli
Founder, World Competitiveness Center
Professor Emeritus at IMD and at the University of Lausanne

Towards a Sustainable World is a last appeal by a talented, thoughtful man whose life was devoted to understanding our deeply troubled world and what must be done about it. It deserves the attention of concerned people at every level of society.

Dee W. Hock
Founder and CEO Emeritus, Visa Inc.
Author of *One From Many*

In *Towards a Sustainable World: 3 Paradigm Shifts to Achieve,* Bernard Lietaer shares an optimistic vision of a sustainable future in which efficiency and resilience are balanced in our natural, economic, and information systems. The bold path forward outlined in the book provides the basis for important conversations that need to occur if our global society is to survive in an increasingly complex world. This is an important read for anyone interested in how humanity can navigate our technological future.

Michael Soskil
Co-Author of *Teaching in the Fourth Industrial Revolution*
2017-2018 Pennsylvania Teacher of the Year
2016 Global Teacher Prize Top-10 Finalist

For a small book, Bernard Lietaer's *Towards a Sustainable World* contains an outstandingly rich set of arguments, examples, principles, guidelines, and recommendations for ultimately achieving the transformation needed for the long-term survival of humanity. In a world out of balance, it is quite urgent for us to take action in the direction of the three paradigm shifts proposed by Bernard Lietaer and his colleagues.

Wilhelm Krull
General Secretary, Volkswagen Foundation

In his book, *Towards a Sustainable World,* Bernard Lietaer articulates the case for sustainability and the alignment of the pursuit of environmental and social benefits. He demonstrates that sustainability is of value when employed as a sufficient and strategic framework for creation of value, enhancement of organizational methods for sustainability, and real innovation.

As the reader discovers – what has changed is the context within which the world today operates and the shift that is imperative. The author encourages and iterates a positive message that the shift toward the pursuit of ethical, sustainable capitalism is on the rise. It is and will be full of integrity, balance and thoughtfulness. Most importantly, the positive message from the author is that he has faith we will get it right before it is too late.

I highly recommend Lietaer's thoughtful book as a must-read to understand the shift taking place and as a guide to a creative, sustainable future.

Jennifer Long
President Biolley Farms, Costa Rica

I never had the pleasure of meeting Bernard Lietaer in person; but of course, his name is well known to me. I know that he has been in regular contact with WIR Bank for many years. Be it in personal talks at our headquarters in Basel, by phone or very often via email. The constant dialogue was extremely valuable for both sides. On the one hand, Lietaer found answers to his questions about the practical implementation of a complementary system with its own currency. On the other hand, we learned from him where exactly the problems with the Euro resided and how and where Silvio Gesell's idea and basic ideas could flow into the problem solution. In addition, we received a critical view of the WIR system and its role in the future from an internationally recognized economist, who had dealt with the topic of complementary systems for decades.

Sustainability – this term already appears in the title of Bernard Lietaer's new book – is also the basic idea behind our WIR system. For 85 years we have been committed to promoting small and medium-sized enterprises in Switzerland, which form the backbone of the Swiss economy. And we will continue to do so, contributing to the prosperity of our country. We very much hope that Bernard Lietaer's book will provide valuable impulses for a more sustainable economy.

Bruno Stiegeler
President, WIR Bank, Switzerland

In our current challenging worldwide environment where we face a new kind of political leader embracing nationalist objectives empowered by minor and well-organized social activist groups and old corrupted political parties that are mainly concerned with maintaining their political power above dire social needs, worldwide corporate organizations are under huge pressures from shareholders for immediate and short term profit increase on a year to year basis.

The academic environment is mainly focused on innovation, competition and all the technological revolution impact we are facing in every discipline. But the subjects mentioned in Bernard Lietaer´s book are not considered as they should be in order to build and reinforce a "SUSTAINABLE WORLD."

The paradigms in Bernard´s book are a great contribution to take into consideration, and they should begin in academia and should be implemented from the very beginning of the education cycle, high school or Junior High.

Sustainability and Efficiency must be included in the Strategic Planning Process of our businesses and government environments, prioritizing these implementations as Corporate/Government objectives for a Superior Value Delivery in our world.

Federico G. Lepe
President, International Logistics Commission
Council of Industrial Chambers, Mexico

During his life, Bernard Lietaer was one of the world's most original thinkers about the financial system. I learned a great deal from him and I respected his work. I was surprised and very saddened to hear about his death, since the world needs his ideas now more than ever.

Dennis Meadows
Author of *The Limits to Growth*
Member, The Club of Rome

Towards a Sustainable World

3 Paradigm Shifts To Achieve

Bernard Lietaer
With Helga Preuß, Marek Hudon,
Dieter Legat, Kristof de Spiegeleer,
Cary Sherburne

www.sustainable-world.ch

Design and layout by Robin Wrighton

Printed by DGS GmbH, www.BuchDrucker.at

ISBN: 978-3-200-06527-7

Published by: Delta Institute – Dieter Legat E.U.
Schoenburgstrasse 13/12
A 1040 Vienna/Wien, Austria

CONTENTS

FIGURES

Dear Reader

I have spent my entire professional life in the monetary world. Since 1987, I have developed, tested and implemented complementary currencies in many projects all over the world. This work, and the entire concept of monetary systems, has even more relevance in the turbulent times we find ourselves in as the second decade of the new century comes to a close. And as my life comes to a close, I am compelled to share with you, dear reader, my thoughts about how we, as the human race, can and must address the critical challenges that are facing us – and indeed, threatening our survival.

Today, I see mankind facing enormous challenges, including three that are overwhelming:

- **Climate Change:** It is happening and will bring drastic changes to how we can live and survive. It is truly a climate emergency and we are rapidly approaching the point of no return.
- **Refugees:** The Organization for Economic Co-operation and Development (OECD) forecasts that Europe must cope with hundreds of millions of migrating people. We can also expect similar moves worldwide, driven both by climate change and political and economic conditions in their home countries.
- **Monetary Stability:** our present monetary system is staggering from crash to crash.

Yet, I am and remain optimistic. I do believe that human beings have always faced challenges that stretched beyond the limits of their present capacity. Such challenges forced humans to grow and develop to the next phase in their evolution, ultimately navigating the paradigm shifts they faced. We are in a period now where we must enter another phase in our evolution, and this time we must simultaneously navigate three critical paradigm shifts.

So, that is our situation today: we face challenges the likes of which we have never seen before. Yet, I see the opportunity for mankind to learn and develop. The opportunity lies in going through three paradigm shifts in one sweep, something mankind has never had to do before. These paradigm shift imperatives are the subjects of this book. We must move:

- From Aristotle's linear cause-effect to a more balanced Taoist paradigm;
- From a patrifocal to a more matrifocal paradigm; and
- From centrally-owned to personally-owned information.

As my life draws to a close, I write this last book to show that, despite the severity of the challenges we face, there is no reason for despair. Instead, I challenge the people of this world — each single individual – to get up and move (even better: lead) through these three paradigm shifts. It is the only path to a sustainable future.

I wish you all success!

Bernard Lietaer, January 10, 2019

EDITOR'S NOTE: Bernard Lietaer passed away on 4 February 2019 following an illness, which he thought he had overcome.

To the Leaders of Our World

You are responsible for a sustainable world.

- **Lead to sustainability.**
- **Lead to balance matrifocal and patrifocal values.**
- **Lead human information to personal ownership.**

1

The Story of This Book

The story of how this book was written is very special.

On January 9 and 10, in Hoyerhagen, Germany, Bernard dictated the foreword of the book and then explained in detail to his partner, Helga Preuss, and to Dieter Legat what should be the content of the book. The book was to be his legacy, the essence of his life's work, what he wanted to leave behind for mankind as his call to action.

The three paradigm shifts he considered vital for humanity to bring our world back to sustainability were to be the focus of the book – based on the law of sustainability of living systems, which he had discovered with his friends Robert E. Ulanowicz and Sally J. Goerner.

He also determined that Marek Hudon, his successor as teacher, should edit the manuscript and suggest some references; and Helga should make sure that every word was precisely in his frame of thinking. Kristof de Spiegeleer, expert in information systems, should finalize, from Bernard's notes, the content of Paradigm 3. Cary Sherburne, experienced editor, was asked to help in transforming the manuscript into text easy to read by lay people, and Dieter Legat was to be the scribe of the team.

So we arrived, guided by Bernard, at this book, his last message to humanity.

Thank you, Bernard, for allowing us to serve you.

Helga Preuß, Marek Hudon, Kristof de Spiegeleer,
Dieter Legat, Cary Sherburne.

EDITOR'S NOTE: Helga was Bernard's companion for years; Marek is Professor at Université Libre de Bruxelles (ULB), Belgium; Kristof is CEO of THREEFOLD, a leading high tech company using a complementary Token currency worldwide; Dieter is a retired Hewlett Packard manager and top management consultant, a friend of Bernard's for more than 40 years; Cary is Senior Editor at WhatTheyThink, a media resource focused on the analog-to-digital transformations several industries are undergoing, as well as a marketing consultant and author.

For more information about Bernard Lietaer and achieving the paradigm shifts described in this book, and to join the global conversation, please visit https://sustainable-world.ch.

2

At a Glance

Just a few years ago, we enjoyed life and the future looked brilliant. Men walked on the moon. We were getting diseases under control. Democracy spread out all over the world. Women's' rights expanded. We had peace in most countries of the world. Prosperity was growing. The future for our children looked bright. We were proud of what we would leave behind for them.

Today, the joy of life seems to be gone for many. Now, fear dominates the world. There are threats wherever we look. Will climate change turn our homelands into deserts – or submerge them in rising oceans? Will thousands of immigrants so dramatically change the economic climate that it destroys our chances of maintaining good jobs? Will our economy fall apart? Will our savings disappear? Will a new world balance of power destroy our countries? Will our children have a safe future? Will we ever heal the massive cultural and political divides that seem to be driving us into ever more conflicted tribes?

These threats feel real, don't they? It often seems like there is nothing we can do, that all that's left for us is to be afraid of the future.

This book emphatically says NO, that is not true. It says that we can turn things around. But in order to do so, we humans must all change the way we view our world through three simultaneous paradigm shifts that will help us define what is really going wrong with the world, what to do about it and how we can drive the required changes, as individuals and as participants in families, communities and various organizations.

Paradigm shift, defined:

A situation in which the usual and accepted way of doing or thinking about something changes completely.[1]

First: we need put on new glasses and look at our world through a different lens. We must begin to see it in a different light. We must view our world as a large living being consisting of many smaller living beings[2] – self-organizing life forms. Indeed, we as individuals are self-organizing life forms, or systems, as are our families, our societies, forests, the sea, our monetary systems, our countries, our economies... This is NOT scientific nonsense – it is simply a different way of looking at our world.

Second: We must view these systems as nature does. We must recognize that both our well-being and our future depends on how sustainable these life forms or systems are. We must grow to understand that the root cause of our problems is that many of these systems are not sustainable any longer in their current form. And we must fully grasp what we need to do to return them to sustainability.

Third: we must focus on changing a few vital things that are the root cause of our troubles – not on the larger scope of world-improving policies. Programs addressing the climate emergency, fixing our economy, keeping refugees out…all

---

1 https://dictionary.cambridge.org/us/dictionary/english/paradigm-shift

2 Scientists call these "systems."

these address symptoms, not the root causes. And focusing on these is not effective or efficient… it's also overwhelming.

Rather, we must address the root cause, which is one single problem: our world is not sustainable because it is out of balance.

This is the call to action of this book. It is not written to be read and discussed by a few scientists or activists. It is for the entire world, for every human being, for all leaders in this world, wherever they may be. For you, our reader. For you, the top politicians in the U.S., in China, in Europe – anywhere in the world. For you, the business leaders. For you, the spiritual leaders:

It is incumbent on all of us to bring our world back into balance and move forward to sustainability. Only then will fear about the future be history.

This book shows us how.

Change agents have courage – a certain fearlessness about the future.

~ Jack Welch, former CEO of General Electric

3

The Language of the New Paradigms

The major problems of our time –the threat of nuclear war, the devastation of our natural environment, our inability to cope with poverty and starvation around the world… are all different facets of one single crisis, which is essentially a crisis of perception. It derives from the fact that most of us – and especially our large social institutions –subscribe to the concepts of an outdated world view.

~ Fritjof Capra, Scientist, Author, Educator and Activist

Every profession has its own special language for its field of work, its paradigm, the way it views its field and the world around it. Fire fighters, medical doctors, airplane pilots – all have specific terms to describe types of challenges, obstacles to overcome and actions to take, terms that are likely not understood outside of their respective professions. Clear meanings are prerequisites for a paradigm. This is required for people to describe, share, and communicate.

Just as each profession has its own language, so, too, do our new paradigms. This is the global language that will help everyone understand the dangers we face, and what we can do about them. The terms used in our special language are listed and defined here in brief, and in more detail in this book.

In order to begin this discussion using a common language, we have defined key terms important to the understanding of each of the three required paradigm shifts. They will act as a reference point as readers proceed through the book.

General

- **Paradigm:** A framework of thought, concepts, methods, causal connections.
- **Yin and Yang:** The principle that all things exist as inseparable and contradictory opposites; for example, female and male, dark and light, old and young.[3]

Paradigm Shift 1: From Aristotle to Tao

Living Systems

- **Living systems[4]:** Self-organizing life forms that interact with their environment.
- **Flow:** These living systems are maintained by flows of information, energy and matter. If the flow is hindered, the system is in trouble.
- **Network View of Living System:** This approach views systems as consisting of a network of elements interacting through flows of information, energy, matter.
- **Ecosystem:** The entirety of a system and all the systems with which it interacts.
- **Efficiency of a Living System:** A living system's capacity to perform in a sufficiently organized and efficient manner in order to maintain its integrity over time.

3 https://www.ancient.eu/Yin_and_Yang

4 https://en.wikipedia.org/wiki/Living_systems

- **Resilience of a Living System:** Its reserve of flexible fallback positions and diversity of actions that can be used to meet changing conditions and the innovation required for ongoing development and evolution.
- **Sustainability of a Living System:** The quality of being able to continue to function over a period of time.[5]
- **Viability:** The ability to live, grow, and develop.[6]

Cause-effect Logic

- **Causality:** The connection between cause and effect.
- **Linear Causality:** One cause leads directly to one effect.
- **Linear System:** A system that responds to one cause (trigger) with one effect.
- **Non-linear System:** A system that responds to one cause (trigger) with multiple and changing effects.

Monetary System

- **Monetary System:** A system, which organizes the flow of money.
- **Monetary System, Conventional:** The official monetary system, used worldwide, independent of the political orientation of countries. It consists of a set of policies, frameworks, and institutions by which the government creates money in an economy. Such institutions include the mint, the central bank, treasury, and other financial institutions.[7]

---

5 https://dictionary.cambridge.org/dictionary/english/sustainability

6 https://www.merriam-webster.com/dictionary/viability

7 https://www.intelligenteconomist.com/monetary-systems

- **Monetary System, Complementary:** An additional monetary system, complementing the conventional system (not an alternative system).
- **Demurrage Currency:** a currency in which the value of units of currency is designed to fall over time at a fixed rate.

Paradigm Shift 2: Towards a More Balanced Matrifocal/Patrifocal Partnership

- **Matrifocal:** A matrifocal family or society is one where females play a leading role and males play a less important role.
- **Matrifocality:** A focus on resilience and longer-term results.
- **Patrifocal:** A patrifocal family or society is one where males play a leading role and females play a less important role.
- **Patrifocality:** A focus on efficiency and short-term results.

Paradigm Shift 3: Towards More Personal Ownership of Information

- **Centralization of Information:** Information stored and access managed by one central organization.
- **Decentralization of Information:** Information stored and managed by each member of a network.
- **Distributed Information:** The same information resides with each user. If it is not, one or a few users have it.
- **Proprietary Information:** Information that is not public knowledge and that is viewed as the property of the holder.

- **Personal Information:** Information or an opinion, including information or an opinion forming part of a database, whether true or not, and whether recorded in a material form or not, about an individual whose identity is apparent, or can reasonably be ascertained, from the information or opinion.
- **Private Information:** Information that a user wishes to keep from public view. Credit card, social security and financial account numbers, along with passwords to websites and other venues, are commonly kept private.

We understand that these terms are not necessarily in common use. But by defining them here, it will help our readers to better understand the paradigm shifts this book presents.

Equipped with this language, let us now take a look at each of these three paradigm shifts, which we consider essential to bringing balance back into our world and moving us towards a sustainable future.

4

Paradigm Shift 1: From Aristotle to Tao

Like all major transitions in human history, the shift from a linear to a circular economy will be a tumultuous one. It will feature heroes and pioneers, naysayers and obstacles, and moments of victory and doubt. If we persevere, however, we will put our economy back on a path of growth and sustainability.

~ Frans van Houten, CEO at Royal Phillips

Sustainability: The Goal of Living Systems

Living systems are life forms maintained by flows of information, energy and matter, interacting with their environment and organizing themselves. Forests are living systems, as are animals, businesses, societies and, of course, human beings.

Such life forms have one overall goal: to remain healthy and alive today and tomorrow; in other words, their goal is sustainability.

The Vital Question: How Can We Ensure Living Systems Remain Viable, and Thus, Sustainable?

As we moved forward in history, the more we learned about our world and ourselves, the more we learned that our own survival depends on keeping living systems in balance and sustainable: The forests that produce the oxygen we need to breathe; the banks that provide us with money; the governments that provide us with security; health care systems that come to our aid if needed; businesses who pay us salaries to live on – just to name a few.

Aristotle's Logic: Only a Partial Answer

A few hundred years B.C., Aristotle gave us a great gift: the principles of logic. We have used these principles ever since to help us make decisions. They are based on "if – then" assumptions, like:

"If I kick a ball well, then it will land in the goal," or as business managers: "If we hire more sales people, then we will sell more product."

Fig. 1: Aristotle, Greek Philosopher, 384-322 BC. Originator of linear causality.

Logic experts call this kind of cause-effect logic linear: one cause leads directly to one effect.

Unfortunately for life forms (living systems), Aristotle's logic model often fails to define reality: the interactions we confront in life are seldom linear. Instead, they often appear in loops – forward or backward in the chain of events, often resulting in unforeseen consequences.

In Figure 2, we see the direct line between cause (kicking the ball or hiring more salespeople) with the expected effect (ball in goal or more sales). But the non-linear causality shown on the right is more likely what we will see in real living systems. There are loops and conditions that amplify, hinder or delay the expected outcome. Certainly, we can expect more orders if we add more salespeople. But more orders can create unexpected consequences, such as backlogs and delays in delivery that can have an adverse effect on whether or not we actually get those orders – whether customers will accept those delays and longer lead times. This is referred to as non-linear causality by logic experts and is typically more common in living systems than the more simplistic linear causality.

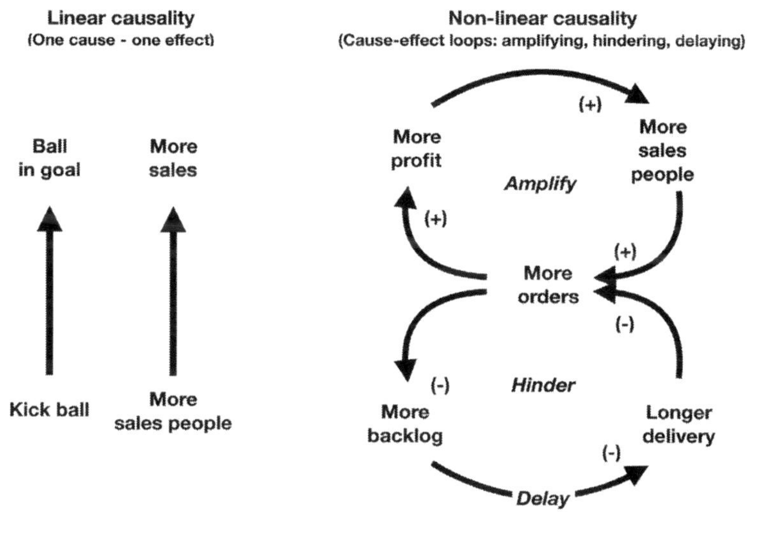

Fig. 2: Linear causality is "straight." Non-linear is "circular."

Real living systems, of course, are much more inter-looped than our simplified example in Figure 2, more like what is depicted in Figure 3. Here we see that the decline of forest cover on Negros Island (an island in the Philippines) is the result of several intertwined cause-effect loops.[8] It is much more representative of actual living systems than the simple loops showing in Figure 2.

In such cases, Aristotle's linear logic applies to cause-effect between two nodes – but not to cause-effect relationships within the entire living system.

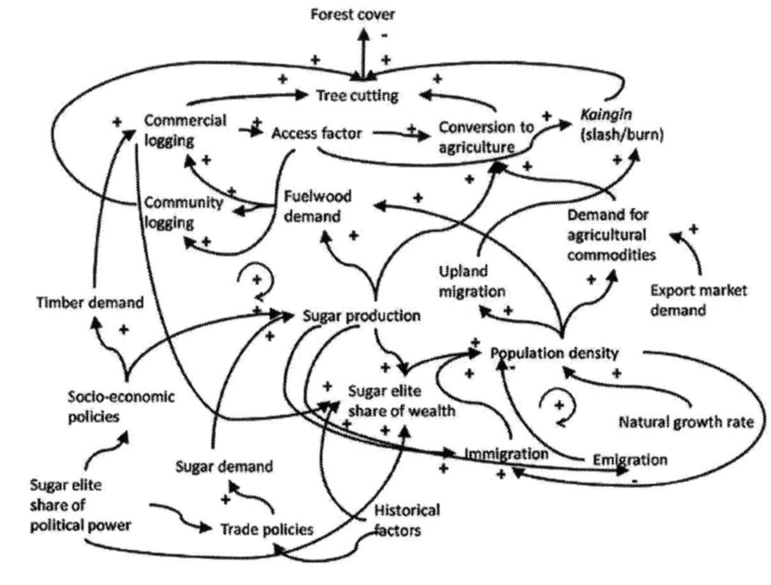

Fig. 3: In living systems non-linear (circular) causality prevails.

Our illustration shows a causal loop diagram depicting forest cover decline on Negros Island, generated by researchers from the World Wildlife Fund. Two primary positive feedback loops are embedded in the model: one caused by social-economic policies and the second one from population density.

8 https://www.researchgate.net/figure/Causal-loop-diagram-depicting-forest-cover-decline-on-Negros-Island-generated-by_fig1_45267560

The Law of Sustainability for Living Systems

Recognizing these limitations of Aristotle's logic, Bernard looked for an answer to the question: "What makes a living system sustainable?" with Sally J. Goerner and Robert E. Ulanowicz, (both leading scientists).In 2008, they presented their joint results: scientific proof that living systems must reach a balance between efficiency and resilience to attain sustainability.[9]

The law of sustainability
To reach optimum sustainability, a living system must balance its efficiency and resilience.

Figure 4 is a graph from the book, *Money and Sustainability – the Missing Link*,[10] p.80. It shows sustainability as the balance between resilience and efficiency. Bernard and his friends found that all natural ecosystems operate within a window of viability around the optimal point of this balance. In other words, the optimal point is the ideal balance between efficiency and resilience. The window of viability defines the acceptable range before the balance is tipped too far one way or the other – reducing the system's sustainability.

Everything in life … has to have balance.
~ Donna Karan, Fashion designer

Complementary Forces

Both resilience and efficiency are related to the levels of diversity and connectivity found in the network, but in opposite directions:

---

9 Sally J. Goerner, Bernard Lietaer, Robert E. Ulanowicz: "Quantifying economic sustainability: Implications for free-enterprise theory, policy and practice", 28 August 2009.

10 See chapter "Four Books, One Article."

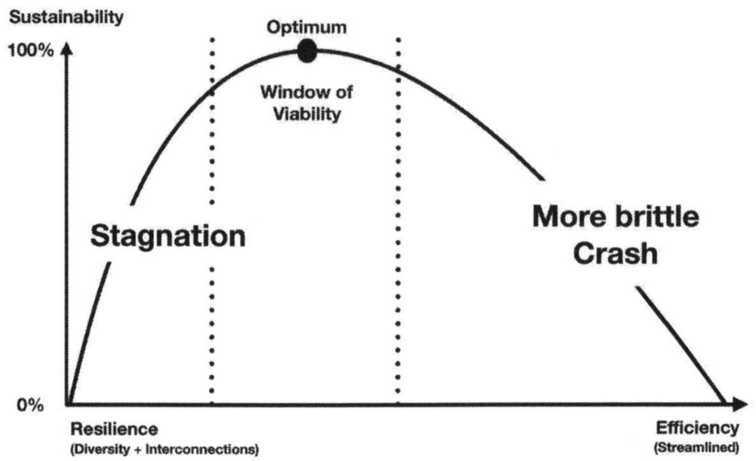

Fig. 4: Law of sustainability: Living systems are sustainable by balancing resilience and efficiency.

A well-woven multiplicity of connections and diversity plays a positive role in resilience, for example, because additional options help the system rebound from the loss or disruption of one or more pathways or nodes.

Yet living systems also require efficient end-to-end circulation of products in order to properly catalyze crucial processes at all levels of the whole. Redundant pathways and excess connections hinder throughput efficiency, leading to stagnation that erodes vitality.

In short, resilience and efficiency are essentially complementary forces because the streamlining that increases efficiency automatically reduces resilience. In general, then, greater efficiency means less resilience; and, conversely, greater resilience means less efficiency. The challenge is to find the balance that defines the window of viability.

Scientific details on the law of sustainability

The long-term maintenance of vitality appears to rest heavily on two structure-related attributes:

1) Efficiency: the network's capacity to perform in a sufficiently organized and efficient manner as to maintain its integrity over time… and,

2) Resilience: its reserve of flexible fallback positions and diversity of actions that can be used to meet the exigencies of novel disturbances and the novelty needed for on-going development and evolution.

… The underlying mathematics are sufficiently well-behaved that there exists only a single maximum for any given network system. Interestingly enough, since optimal sustainability is situated slightly toward the resilience side, the resulting asymmetry suggests that resilience plays a grater role in optimal sustainability than does efficiency.

From Sally J. Goerner, Bernard Lietaer, Robert E. Ulanowicz: "Quantifying economic sustainability: Implications for free-enterprise theory, policy and practice," 28 August 2009.

Economic Viability

In their paper, Bernard and his colleagues wrote: "The basic idea is that the same laws of growth and development apply both to natural flow systems and economic ones. … It is our hope that the new ability to define and measure healthy development in complex flow systems … can help provide a solid empirical/mathematical basis for the more accurate diagnosis of how to build and maintain economic vitality being advanced by a wide array of activists, from micro-credit banker Mohammed Yunus to natural capitalism economist Paul Hawkins."

So it is said, for him who understands Heavenly joy, life is the working of Heaven; death is the transformation of things. In stillness, he and the yin share a single Virtue; in motion, he and the yang share a single flow.

~ Zhuangzi, The Complete Works of Chuang Tzu

The Tao View: Balanced Forces

So, we see that Aristotle's cause-effect logic leaves much to be desired in the analysis of complex living systems, whether natural, human or economic. To supplement Aristotle, then, and to provide a broader understanding of living systems, we turn to the Tao view.

Taoists conceived that all forces exist in complementary pairs – like heaven-earth, fire-water, inhaling-exhaling, pulling-pushing, life-death, etc. As Figure 5 shows with respect to the Taoist view, the same applies to human behavior.

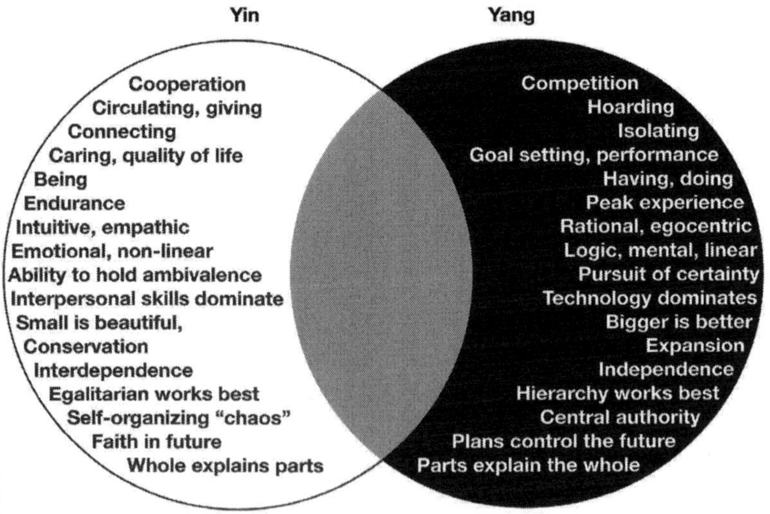

Fig. 5: Yin and Yang – Opposing forces in balance.

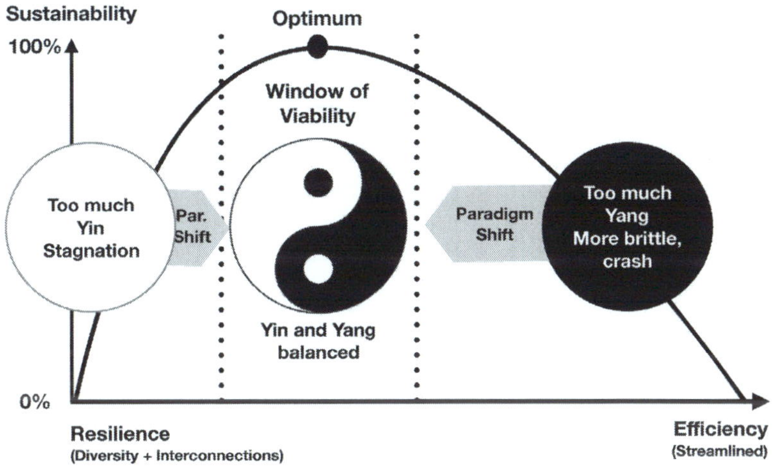

Fig. 6: The law of sustainability confirms the Yin and Yang principle.

The key message is that – although each side of the pair is obviously a separate force, the pair also forms part of a single ultimate unity, the Tao, and therefore each needs its opposite in order to arrive at wholeness. In other words: it is the balance between the two that matters, not one or the other.

The Yin/Yang symbol illustrates this by showing as the core of each side an element of the other (represented by the small dots in Figure 6).

Five principles are essential for the Yin/Yang view:

1. Both are equal.
2. Each opposes the other.
3. Both depend on each other.
4. Both counterbalance each other.
5. Both must balance to achieve a healthy, harmonious situation.

Yin, Yang and the Law of Sustainability

The law of sustainability of living systems says exactly that – with resilience representing the Yin and efficiency the Yang:

1. Both are equally essential for system sustainability. A living system MUST care for both. In autumn, a bear must feed both for today (efficiency) and for the coming winter hibernation (resilience). In a family, you must care both for today and tomorrow; ignoring either of them leads to disaster.
2. Efficiency and resilience oppose each other. An example is how you decide to spend your money: do you spend all your money today or do you put some aside for tomorrow? Or as a business leader, you might need to decide between spending money to pay a bonus now or invest that money in developing new product that will benefit the future of the company.
3. The two depend on each other. Some refer to this dependency as "rooted in each other," A bear cannot stop feeding for today and only feed for tomorrow. A company cannot stop product development for short-term profit reasons without harming its longer-range survival. In other words, you need yin to have yang, and yang to have yin.
4. Resilience and efficiency counterbalance each other. Ideally, the balance is 50–50; but if the balance is off, then one will have more than 50% while the other has less than 50%.
5. It requires a balance between Yin (resilience) and Yang (efficiency) to achieve optimal sustainability for the living system. Too much emphasis on resilience (Yin)

leads to stagnation. Too much emphasis on efficiency makes the system too brittle and leads it to crash.[11]

This is the Root Cause of Our Problems

This is the root cause of our problems in the world today: most, if not all, of the living systems we are using, influencing or leading are not in balance between efficiency and resilience anymore. Instead, we have pushed them or let them fall to the right side of the curve of sustainability, striving for efficiency while ignoring resilience – resulting in loss of sustainability. Monocultures are an example of this. Monocultures are the cultivation of a single crop within a given area or the concentration of a single type or style of a thing within a living system.

We drive towards monocultures to achieve efficiency, ignoring the needed balance with resilience: in forestry, in our monetary system, even in fashion (fashion chain outlets everywhere offer the same model, very boring for fashionistas, but efficient for purchasing) – wherever we look.

Hey, is There Anything New Here? No and Yes

No. Intuitively, you and I already understand this need for balance. You know that to sell a used car at a good price, you also need to keep it in good condition (resilience) while driving it efficiently.

And Yes. Mankind ignores this law, often behaving as if it does not apply. Two examples:

- In the monetary system, we spend and borrow money as if there were no risk in the future. We have adopted the principle of enjoy now – pay later, even to the degree

[11] https://www.ancient.eu/Yin_and_Yang

that our countries go into debt for us, debt that our children and grandchildren will have to pay back.

- In the travel system, flying for low prices has become part of the traveler's lifestyle. In 2015, for example, Swiss citizens flew 9,000 kilometers (about 5,600 miles) per person per year, a growth of 57% over 2010. About 80% of these trips were for vacation purposes. In Switzerland, air travel is responsible for 18% of man-made impact on the climate. Everyone knows that flying places a heavy load on the environment. Still we continue, often just finding convenient excuses for doing so.[12]

Some Real-World Examples

Let's take a look at some real-world examples of how we can move living systems forward and shift the paradigm to more balance – for ourselves, and the world. More specifically, we'll take a look at examples of paradigms that must be left behind to bring balance and sustainability to the world.

Example 1: Shifting Toward More Mixed Woodland[13]

Our approach to managing forests is a good example that illustrates how monocultures over-emphasize efficiency and how minimizing monocultures brings a living system forward to balance, and thus, forward to sustainability:

The Paradigm to Leave Behind: Myopic Focus on Efficiency

In Portugal in the past, when reforesting abandoned farm territory or burned areas of forest, preference was given to

---

12 Helmut Stalder, NZZ (*Neue Zuercher Zeitung*), March 20, 2019)

13 http://www.geoengineeringmonitor.org/2018/11/fire-and-plantations-in-portugal

monoculture: pine or eucalyptus trees were typically planted. Both grow quickly and provide raw material for the local paper industry. Even the European Union subsidized this approach.

However, pine trees catch fire quickly; and eucalyptus trees, originally from Australia, are a powerful accelerator of fire. Their bark has a high resin content so that these trees catch fire instantly. They practically explode, with pieces of burning bark flying hundreds of meters, setting the next section of forest on fire.

As a result of the monoculture approach to reforestation, Portugal paid a high price. Large areas of forest burnt down, and many people died or were injured. In the end, the monoculture sacrificed resilience for efficiency, and the system was out of balance.

Fig. 7: The price to pay for Eucalyptus monoculture (Portugal).

Balancing Efficiency with Resilience: Back to Mixed Woodland

Now Portugal has reverted to a mixed woodland strategy, with local species of trees. In addition, they plant shrubs and bushes that prevent drying of the forest floor in periods of drought.

By reverting to mixed woodlands, their forest systems are pushed forward to sustainability even though this project will take a full generation to complete.

Example: Rubber Tree Plantations

Fig. 8: Just rubber trees – no others.

Rubber tree plantations typically are monocultural, for efficiency reasons. Nature detests monocultures and does anything possible to bring them back to high sustainability, attacking with insects and fungi of various types.

In return, we try to fight back with chemicals, aiming at keeping these forests on the efficiency side of the law of sustainability.

This quote from *Advances in Chemicals*[14] shows how some chemicals are used to keep rubber plantation monocultures in production: "The future of natural rubber is very bright, as it is more important than synthetics in European markets and supplies over half of world needs, in spite of subsidies to synthetics. However, rubber trees are susceptible to a number of diseases. Mildew is the most serious leaf disease in Africa and the Far East but is being effectively treated with sulfur dusts. South American leaf blight is controlled by spraying with Dithane. Phytophthora foliage blight is increasing but is being controlled by Dithane and Vancide. Tapping panel disease, also caused by Phytophthora, is increasing, although Orthocide and other treatments are proving effective."

But what damage do these chemicals ultimately cause to our environment and thus, to humans? Unfortunately, we may not know the full impact for some time.

Rubber trees originated in Brazil. In the 1800s, it was illegal to export rubber trees or seeds, but they were smuggled out anyway. These were used to create rubber plantations in Asia and other parts of the world. In their native environment, rubber trees grew dispersed among a mixed forest environment. If one tree became diseased, it was less likely to infect another one growing at some distance. But when rubber plantations were established in South and Southeast Asia, with row after row of rubber trees, these trees became more susceptible to disease. In many ways, this is a disaster waiting to happen, much as the potato famine in Ireland in the 1840s resulted in a

14 https://pubs.acs.org/doi/abs/10.1021/ba-1955-0013.ch007?src=recsys

disaster that caused mass starvation, disease and emigration, with potato blight rapidly spreading from plant to plant. In rubber plantations, a disease known as white root rot, first reported in 1904 in Singapore, poses the greatest threat to the world supply of rubber. According to Wikipedia, "White root rot has now become the most threatening root disease of the rubber tree in both Asian and African Continents which supply 98% of the natural rubber to the world market. In Indonesia alone, the affected area is more than 80,000 hectares [nearly 200,000 acres]. As a whole, 5% to 10% of cultivated lands lie in bare patches due to this deadly disease."[15]

Towards Mixed Culture

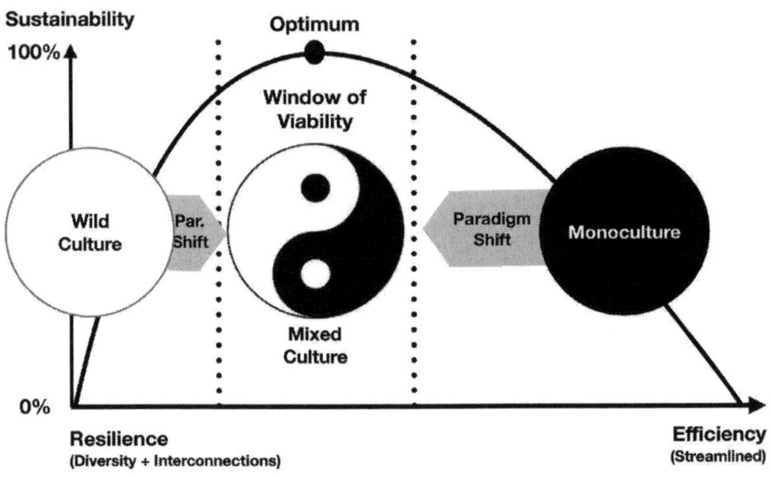

Fig. 9: Mixed forest culture fulfills the law of sustainability.

[15] https://en.wikipedia.org/wiki/Rigidoporus_microporus#White_root_rot_of_rubber, April 2019

For efficiency – low cost of maintenance and harvesting – monocultures are undoubtedly the solution.

However, we can see from these examples that monocultures violate the law of sustainability. Driven by focus on efficiency, they weaken resilience and thus drive their systems towards collapse.

So far, we have looked at living systems in nature (forests and other plantations are living systems, of course). Now let us look – in another example – at a man-made system: our money.

As you will see, the same law applies: our conventional monetary system is a monoculture and therefore unstable by definition.

Example 2: Towards Dual Monetary Systems

Today's Monetary System: A Key Driver of Productivity and Wealth[16]

We should give credit to the conventional monetary system for having given birth to the industrial age, with both its positive and negative effects.

Money experts call conventional money "Fiat money" (referring to the first sentence in the Bible "fiat lux" – light out of nothing), a currency that in itself has no intrinsic value, but rather has value because a government maintains its values.

It has spawned a quantum leap in scientific knowledge and the most materially productive civilization in the history of mankind. It has also been an extraordinary wealth-producing mechanism, and we hope that it can continue to play that role in an evolving monetary ecosystem.

---

16 See Bernard Lietaer's book *Money and Sustainability – The Missing Link,* Report from the Club of Rome – EU Chapter, 2012, written with Christian Arnsperger, Sally J. Goerner and Stefan Brunnhuber

However, Monocultural and Efficiency Focused

However, it is definitely monocultural and an extremely efficiency-focused Yang construct whose interest feature encourages accumulation and concentration of wealth in the form of money, and whose necessary scarcity promotes competition amongst its users. Here are some of its effects that fly in the face of the law of sustainability:

- It amplifies the business cycle of boom and bust, which is detrimental to businesses, countries and even banks themselves. Consider the boom-and-bust cycle in Silicon Valley in the late 1990s, or the financial disaster caused by poor lending strategies on the part of financial institutions that caused the 2008 global recession.
- It enforces short-term thinking by the standard practice of discounting future costs or income. This was especially true in the 2008 global recession.
- It enforces exponential growth by the process of compound interest – which is, by definition, unsustainable in a finite world,
- It leads to concentration of wealth, resulting in the middle class disappearing worldwide. This concentration reduces diversity and causes a wide range of social problems.

These features position our conventional monetary system firmly to the far right of our law of sustainability, making it "brittle and easy to crash," as the many bank and stock crashes in past years illustrate.

Complementary Currencies[17] Support a System's Resilience

Whenever a monopoly of Yang currency prevails, the Yin functions tend to be less acknowledged and honored and are systematically starved of resources. In other words, such money systems result in spending more money on the Yang side, and reducing spending on the Yin side.

The solution to establishing a sustainable balance in monetary systems, Bernard always emphasized, lies in – as he called them – complementary currencies. These are agreements within a community to accept something other than conventional currencies as a means of payment.

He was strict about how the term "complementary" should be used: only currencies which aim at supporting a system's resilience or Yin functions should be called "complementary," in the sense of "something that fills up, completes, or makes better or perfect."[18] This is especially the case if there is a social need, but the conventional money system fails to assign money to meet that need – like caring for the elderly, for the sick, welfare in the widest sense, education, etc.

Such currencies:

- Dampen business cycles of boom and bust, supporting sustainability of businesses, countries and even banks.
- Support longer term thinking rather than short-term thinking.
- Are interest free, thus do not drive exponential growth.

---

[17] https://en.wikipedia.org/wiki/Complementary_currency

[18] https://www.merriam-webster.com/dictionary/complement

- Bear no interest, or even better, charge fees for storing money, thus discouraging accumulation of money for creating wealth.
- Discourage accumulation of currency, for instance with a "demurrage fee" (see chapter The language of the new paradigms/Monetary system).
- Avoid the ego-centric effects of "money priming."[19]

Cryptocurrencies: Efficiency Focused Yang Currencies[20]

Cryptocurrencies[21] – of which Bitcoin is probably the most well-known example[22] – are digital or virtual currencies that use cryptography and blockchain technology for security to allow for secure payments of online transactions.

Even if a defining feature of such cryptocurrencies is that they are used in parallel with conventional money and are not issued by any central authority, rendering them theoretically immune to government interference or manipulation, by their

---

[19] Priming … refers to activating particular representations or associations in memory just before carrying out an action or task. For example, a person who sees the word ***yellow*** will be slightly faster to recognize the word ***banana***. https://www.psychologytoday.com/intl/basics/priming. "Money-primed people are … more selfish ... much less willing to help … showed a greater preference for being alone. Kahnemann, Daniel; Nobel Prize winner; *Thinking, Fast and Slows,* Penguin Books, p.55.

[20] https://www.investopedia.com/terms/c/cryptocurrency.asp

[21] "Crypto" refers to the fact that various encryption algorithms and cryptographic techniques, such as elliptical curve encryption, public-private key pairs, and hashing functions, are employed.

[22] Bitcoin's success has spawned a number of competing cryptocurrencies, known as "altcoins" such as Litecoin, Namecoin and Peercoin, as well as Ethereum, EOS and Cardano. Today, there are literally thousands of cryptocurrencies in existence, with an aggregate market value of over $120 billion.

very nature they are efficiency-focused Yang currencies. In that sense, the recent announcement of Facebook's new currency LIBRA adds a Yang focused cryptocurrency to the many others that already exist.

However, as Bernard Lietaer pointed out, cryptography and blockchain technology are certainly foundations on which complementary currencies could well be implemented.

Dual Monetary Systems

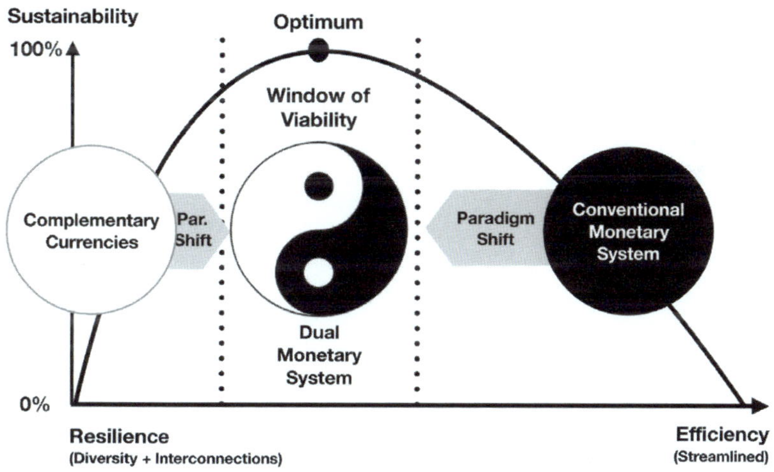

Fig. 10: Complementary currencies balance weaknesses of conventional monetary system.

In a dual monetary system, both the conventional monetary system and one or several complementary currencies co-exist, thus counteracting the weaknesses of the conventional monetary system.

As of 2019, there are more than 4,000 active local dual monetary systems, prototypes of what will actually emerge over the next decade.

Here are five examples for illustration purposes: WIR (Switzerland), Curitiba (Brazil), LETS (worldwide), Ithaca HOURS (USA) and the famous Woergl story.

Example 1: WIR (Switzerland)

Fig. 11: Complementary Currency: WIR Bank, Switzerland.

Created during the financial crisis of the 1930s, the WIR is an important complementary currency in Switzerland. It has become a business-to-business currency with an unheralded dual money banking system behind it.

The story of the WIR's success has its beginnings during the bleak days of the Great Depression. Two Swiss businessmen got together with a dozen or more business associates to decide what they could do to address the financial crisis of the 1930s. They had each received a notice from their respective banks that their credit lines were going to be reduced or eliminated; hence, bankruptcy was inevitable. So, they created a mutual credit system between themselves, inviting their clients and suppliers to join.

The country's banks mounted a massive press campaign to try to squelch this revolutionary idea. The campaign failed, and the system saved the businesses involved.

The value of the WIR is identical to the national currency (Swiss Franc); however, there is a significant difference between the two: the WIR does not bear interest.

Today, approximately 16% of Swiss enterprises use the WIR, with a current volume worth just under 2 billion Swiss Francs in circulation.

Far from representing a disturbing factor for the Swiss National Bank (SNB), the credits created by WIR constitute a support in pursuit of its monetary policy objectives.[23]

Example 2: Curitiba (Brazil)[24]

Fig. 12: Jaime Lerner, Mayor of Curitiba introduced the Curitiba Token.

Garbage was a major problem in Curitiba, the capital of the southeastern state of Paraná, Brazil. Its urban population had mushroomed from 120,000 in 1942 to 2.3 million in 1997. Many of the inhabitants lived in favelas, shantytowns made of cardboard and corrugated metal. Garbage collection trucks could not enter these favelas, as the streets were not wide enough. The garbage piled up, and disease broke out.

Jaime Lerner, who became mayor of Curitiba in 1971, did not have funds to apply customary solutions, such as bulldozing the area or building new streets. Bond measures, further taxation, or federal assistance were simply not options. Another way had to be found.

[23] For more details see the book *Rethinking Money* (written with Jacqui Dunne), p.99 ff.

[24] http://www.lietaer.com/2010/09/the-story-of-curitiba-in-brazil

What Curitiba did have was an abundance of food supplies owing to the fertile lands and tropical climate of southeastern Brazil. It also had a municipal bus system that was underutilized, with many favela residents unable to afford public transportation. Mayor Lerner made use of these local resources to help resolve Curitiba's urban issues.

Large metallic bins were placed at the edge of the favelas. Anyone who deposited a bag full of pre-sorted garbage received a bus token. Those who collected paper and cartons were given plastic chips, exchangeable for parcels of seasonal fresh fruits and vegetables. In addition, a school-based garbage collection program supplied poorer students with notebooks.

Tens of thousands of children responded by picking the neighborhoods clean. Parents made use of the tokens to travel downtown, oftentimes to find jobs. The bus tokens were soon accepted at local markets in exchange for food. In one three-year period, more than 100 schools traded 200 tons of garbage for 1.9 million notebooks. The paper-recycling component alone saved the equivalent of 1,200 trees – each day!

Eventually, more than 70% of Curitiban households became involved in the programs. The 62 poorer neighborhoods alone exchanged 11,000 tons of garbage for nearly a million bus tokens and 1,200 tons of food. Other programs were created to finance the restoration of historic buildings, create green areas, and provide housing – all with methods that placed little or no financial burden on the municipality.

The many initiatives – environmental cleanup, city restoration, job creation, improved education, disease intervention, hunger prevention – were each tackled without having to raise taxes, redistribute wealth, issue bonds, rely on charity or obtain loans from the federal government or organizations such as the World Bank and the International Monetary

Fund (IMF). The improvements burdened no one. Everyone benefited.

The results in purely economic terms are worth noting. From 1975 to 1995, the Gross Domestic Product (GDP) of Curitiba increased an average of 75% more than its parent state of Paraná, and 48% more than the GDP of Brazil as a whole. The average Curitibano earned more than three times the country's minimum wage. If non-traditional monetary gains, such as the exchange of garbage for provisions, are taken into consideration, the real total income for residents was at least 30% higher still. The results in human terms – in the renewal of dignity and hope for a better future – can only be imagined.

Curitiba discovered a means by which to match unmet needs with unused resources. They did so by making use of *complementary currencies* monetary initiatives that did not replace, but rather supplemented, the national currency system. This innovative approach provided much-needed improvements to the local economy. It enabled a developing and formerly impoverished city to empower itself and vastly improve conditions in the remarkable span of a single generation.

Example 3: LETS[25]

The most common dual monetary system in the world today is LETS, an acronym for Local Exchange Trading System. It was invented in the early 1980s in Courtney, Canada, when this town was enduring a 40% local unemployment rate.

There were plenty of things to be done; and a large, skilled labor force willing and needing to work. The missing link was money. Consequently, LETS was created to facilitate

---

[25] More about LETS in Bernard Lietaer's book *Rethinking Money*, written with Jacqui Dunne, p.75

much-needed trade within circuits in local neighborhoods, villages and towns.

Fig. 13: Complementary Currency: ADELAIDE LETS (Australia)

LETS is an example of a mutual credit system whereby currency is created by simultaneous credit and debit in a transaction. It is now operating in many different parts of the world, including Austria, Australia, Belgium, Brazil, Canada, Chile, Colombia, El Salvador, Finland, France, Germany, Hungary, India, Indonesia, Ireland, Israel, Japan, New Zealand, Nigeria, Norway, Poland, South Africa, Switzerland, Thailand and the United States.

Australia has many communities actively trading in LETS. ADELAIDE LETS[26], for example, is a non-profit community exchange system that allows its members to trade goods & services without the need for direct bartering or money.

---

[26] http://www.letsadelaide.org

Example 4: Ithaca HOURS[27]

Ithaca HOURS started in 1991 in Ithaca NY, with each HOUR note worth the equivalent of US$10. Businesses that receive HOURS must spend them on local goods and services, thus promoting the local economy.

In July 2015, a new company called Ithacash moved this complementary currency from the hour notes-based approach to the Ithaca dollar in digital form.

Over 100 local businesses have so far signed up at launch, with some already accepting payments via text message.[28]

Example 5: The Woergl Story

Fig. 14: Rosa and Michael Unterguggenberger.

Woergl is a small community in Austria, located at the railway line connecting Innsbruck and Munich. Back in 1931, some 30 percent of the workforce was unemployed, leaving 200 families absolutely penniless.

The mayor, Michael Unterguggenberger with his wife Rosa, created a solution. They decided to issue labor certificates, which simply became known as "the Woergl."

27 http://www.lightlink.com/hours/ithacahours

28 https://cointelegraph.com/news/ithaca-ny-launches-its-own-digital-currency-to-boost-local-economy

This complementary currency was designed to function solely as a medium of exchange.

Its demurrage[29] charge was applied through a stamp affixed each month at 1 percent of face value.

Like all other such charges, this acted as an incentive to keep the money in circulation. Everybody who was paid in Woergl made sure she or he spent it quickly before the stamp's date expired. (Even taxes were eagerly paid, sometimes even in advance.)

Veronika Spielbichler, custodian of the Unterguggenberger Institute, Woergl, told us:

> *Full employment as consequence of this 'labor value currency' is a famous myth of the Woergl program, which is not really correct. Actually, at the beginning Woergl had 400 unemployed persons, of which 100 found work through the program. Thus, unemployment rate in Woergl dropped by 16% during the 13,5 months in which the program was applied. In the same period in Austria the unemployment rate grew by 19%, so the program resulted in a significant trend reversal for Woergl.*
>
> *Not only did the program generate income for workers: the community's income from the program was also used to fund free meals for unemployed.*

Word of the success of this currency spread like wildfire. Retired French Prime Minister Edouard Daladier even made a special visit to see for himself the miracle of Woergl. Soon more than 200 other towns and villages in Austria wanted to use this system as well.

---

[29] The value of units of currency is designed to fall over time at a fixed rate.

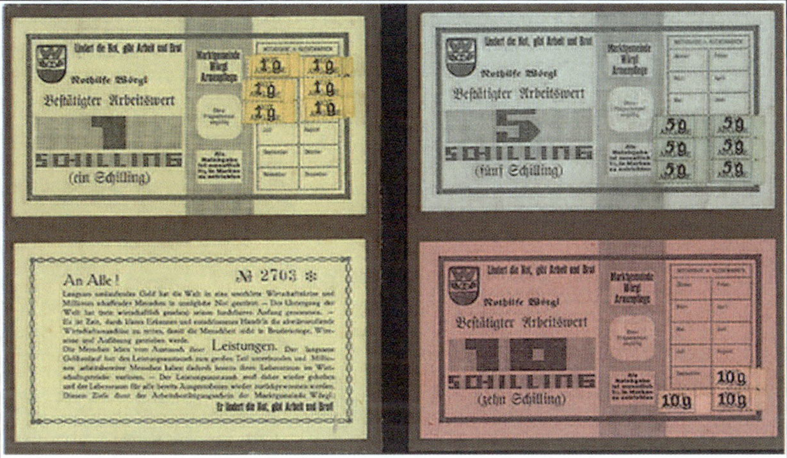

Fig. 15: Complementary Currency: Woergl Schilling.

It was at that point that the Austrian Central Bank panicked and decided to assert its monopoly rights by making it a criminal offence to issue Woergl Schillings.

And Now, It's Your Turn

In this chapter, the intention was to make you aware of the first paradigm shift we must go through: to change our view of how the world works from Aristotle's linear logic to the Tao view. We presented the law of sustainability and illustrated it with two examples: plantations and our monetary system.

Now it's your turn. As Bernard Lietaer said in his letter to you, dear reader: he challenges you to get up and move and lead through this paradigm shift. Go!

You are not helpless; you are not a victim. Instead, you can have an impact, and you can help move our world forward towards a better balance of efficiency and resilience. Here are some steps you can take to help the world along in this important paradigm shift.

First, as an Individual

Just recognizing that our world is out of balance in many living systems and complaining about it is not enough.

Instead, you must go, move and lead through the required paradigm shift yourself, personally. You need to stop exclusive focus on efficiency, like seeking the lowest price, or the highest and fastest gain.

By doing that yourself, you will have gathered the experience to assist, maybe even lead, others towards balancing efficiency and resilience in our systems.

Ultimately, we hope, this leads to a critical mass of adoption that will balance the world and its living systems. For example:

- Recognize how your personal behavior presently prefers to focus on efficiency ("special discount!" "super sale!"). Don't abandon that focus – but balance it with more personal focus on resilience ("bike or car?" "New car or drive the old one longer?")
- When you vote (if your society offers you that luxury), vote for politicians or parties who actually deliver projects balancing resilience and efficiency. Communities that sell (another word with the same meaning is "outsource") their property focus on efficiency; communities that use their properties to add value to citizens focus on resilience. Vote for governments that commit to and deliver a balance of resilience and efficiency in your country or district – not just with cool words, but with actual projects – like banning forest monoculture or fostering complementary currencies.
- In your garden (if you have the luxury of having one), stop the monoculture of lawn. Nature will try to push it back to resilience by bringing in other herbs, and growth

in biodiversity will follow in form of a lot of different plants, insects, birds, etc. If you don't follow the law of sustainability, you might find yourself fighting back with weed killer. Don't do that.

- In your private life and in the organization for which you work: trigger showcase projects focusing on balancing resilience and efficiency and bring them to success.

Second, as Leaders

…of communities, businesses, governments: stop talking, start leading.

- Recognize how you are indoctrinated to lead with a focus on efficiency ("cut cost!" "Improve productivity!")
- Set sustainability of the organizations/systems you own or lead as the single top level and most important goal affecting all your actions and decisions. We are well aware that as leaders of public companies, you are driven almost exclusively by short-term goals in order to keep stock prices high. Viewed through the lens of the law of sustainability, this places focus on the efficiency of your business to the detriment of its resilience. We all instinctively know that ignoring the need for longer term sustainability is deadly for a business. In practical management terms, as a business leader you need both a short-term and a longer-term business plan – one aimed at short-term results, the other one on your business's resilience or longer-term survival. The challenge is to resist the temptation to sacrifice longer-term sustainability for short-term success.

Now is the time for opening the organization you lead to a multitude of individual projects driving towards a better balance between efficiency and diversity.

Yes. This is a Massive Shift

This is a massive paradigm shift, we know. At first sight, it may look easy. But it is not. It asks us to undo a deeply engraved orientation in our world: the focus on quick profit.

Many people have recognized this need already and have described in their books how to go about achieving the required changes.

For complementary currencies, for example, the book Creating Wealth – *Growing Local Economies with Local Currencies* by Gwendolyn Hallsmith and Bernard Lietaer,[30] offers a wide array of examples and suggestions on how to complement conventional with complementary currencies.

Now let us go to the next paradigm shift – perhaps even more difficult to truly achieve, because it means leaving behind cultural values that we have observed for hundreds of years.

---

[30] https://www.amazon.com/gp/product/B005MRA6UK/ref=dbs_a_def_rwt_hsch_vapi_taft_p1_i1

5

Paradigm Shift 2: Towards a Better Matrifocal/Patrifocal Balance

Throughout our everyday life we live in a patrifocal society. That is a world where our corporate jobs, our politics, and our mainstream religions are mainly based on masculine values: domination, hierarchy and control.

~ LotusStudy.com/20082

Sustainable Societies, Defined

A sustainable society satisfies its needs without limiting the prospects of future generations.[31]

Our Values Determine Our Societies' Sustainability

The values we cherish and by which we decide which actions to take determine our societies' sustainability. Some values focus more on our societies' efficiency, others on its resilience.

Focus Both on Efficiency and Resilience of Our Societies

To be sustainable, a society must focus on both. Bernard named them "matrifocal" (focused on a societies' resilience) and patrifocal (focused on its efficiency). These terms perhaps

31 Brundtland Report, quoted in *Money and Sustainability, the Missing Link,* p.33.

seem a little unusual or strange, but Bernard could not find other terms that were clear enough to communicate his meaning:

> *There must be focus on patrifocal values of a societies' efficiency; for instance, to wisely use a societies' resources or to cope with imminent danger like an attack from for a hostile society or of the effects of climate change.*
>
> *Of course, all societies need to also focus on matrifocal values – otherwise vitally important matrifocal functions such as raising and educating children, caring for the elderly, or community and volunteer activities, would not exist. A society completely lacking matrifocal values would therefore soon collapse.*

The ancients envisioned their world in two halves – masculine and feminine. Their gods and goddesses worked to keep a balance of power. Yin and Yang. When male and female were balanced, there was harmony in the world. When they were unbalanced, there was chaos.

~ Dan Brown, The Da Vinci Code

Patrifocal and Matrifocal Values – Both in Women and Men

When you visit an emergency room, you will see people in very bad condition. Every patient injured, broken arms and legs, blood on faces, some sobbing, some crying out. And you will meet nurses. Female and male. They have one of the toughest jobs in the world. On bad days, every minute ambulances bring a new patient in.

When you carefully watch these nurses perform their work, you will become very, very humble. You will see them help, soothe and support patients, care for them – lovingly, yes

– till doctors have time for them, and notice how they really, really care, almost like mothers care for their babies. Men and women – there is no difference in the way good nurses carry out their jobs. Both show this behavior, live these values: Caring like mothers.

At the same time these caretakers perform their duties relentlessly, with high focus on their efficiency. Nurses, then, are a good example of the balance between matrifocal and patrifocal values – a balance between efficiency and resilience.

Each individual person – woman or man – is capable of upholding both these value sets as is demonstrated by our nursing example. Each person finds and experiences her or his personal balancing of patrifocal (focus on efficiency and short-term results) and matrifocal (focus on resilience and longer-term results) values.

It is the blending of the two that makes up the values of a single person.

Out of Balance

In many of our present societies – and often also in our personal values – we are entrenched in patrifocal values. Education and our social environment instruct men to suppress their matrifocal values. To emphasize that exclusive focus, we tend to value patrifocal values higher more highly than matrifocal ones; and in addition at the same time, we coach women to suppress their patrifocal values.

Examples for illustration:

- 28 per cent of women and 45 per cent of men in a recent survey in Germany indicated that they considered women to be less qualified for leadership positions than men.[32]

[32] Study University of Duesseldorf, Nov 2018

- A far too common perception is that when women are stressed, they become emotional and fall apart. But when men are stressed, they remain calm and clear-headed. If you subscribe to either of these beliefs, you're probably going to turn to men, not women, when the pressure is on and an important decision needs to be made.[33]
- Ongoing patrifocal emphasis has resulted in the imbalance we still see today: conflicts wherever you look – wars, invading of land belonging to others, and declaring whole societies as terrorists to justify the right to invade.
- Or in business and politics, we see dominance of patrifocal values reflected in hiring and firing, hostile takeovers, unequal payment for women doing the same jobs as men and even laws that impose prison terms for insulting a leader.
- Some dominantly patrifocal societies even officially permit diminishing societies' resilience by murder, stealing, slavery and rape declaring such actions as a duty to divinity.
- In most countries and businesses, there is still a significant difference in paying salaries for women and men, who are performing the same job.

Not Always So

This was not always so. Up until about 1290 in Europe, for example, women were free to pursue any profession, free to trade, there were no laws defining how women had to dress, and women were the ones who could read and write.

---

https://www.sciencedaily.com/releases/2018/11/181105105401.htm

33 https://www.forbes.com/sites/kathycaprino/2016/05/12/how-decision-making-is-different-between-men-and-women-and-why-it-matters-in-business/#61c0dcb54dcd

Suddenly, then, laws came out forbidding women from participating in professions and trading, limiting women's dresses to simple standards, and they were not allowed to study at universities (until the early 1900s, by the way).

The Required Paradigm Shift

Imagine a Sustainable Society

Imagine a world safe from pollution, a world in which the long-term interests of mankind and our planet temper the short-term interests of business and industry; where conscious cooperation co-exists symbiotically alongside healthy competition; where the proper raising and teaching of our children and caring for our elders is valued and compensated for in equal measure as compared to other forms of employment so vital to our society.

Imagine a world in which there is meaningful work for every human being, together with adequate time for our families, communities and personal pursuits; a world that encourages individual growth as much as it does economic growth; community as it does productivity; conservation as it does consumption. A world that nurtures our spirits and our souls in equal measure to our material needs; a world that fully honors the diversity of all life and the life-affirming aspects of what it is to be fully human in its many myriad shapes and forms.

That is a world where matrifocal and patrifocal values are in balance. And it is ours to achieve.

Matrifocal and Patrifocal Values in Balance

In essence, imagine a world where matrifocal and patrifocal values are in balance, where the two forces are at par. In this balance we recognize that matrifocal energy is of another kind, is as powerful as patrifocal energy and can contribute tremendously to the sustainability of ourselves and our societies.

Bernard told us, for instance, that in his work with students at universities, he personally experienced that persons with matrifocal values apply a different kind of analysis to problems and creation of solutions than patrifocally-oriented persons. Combining the two brings out decisions that are better balanced between resilience and efficiency.

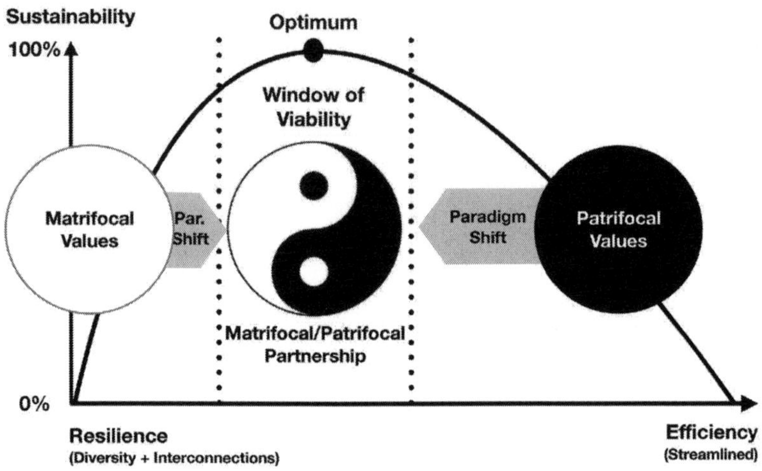

Fig. 16: Balancing matrifocal and patrifocal values ensures sustainability of our societies.

Some Progress – More Required

Actually, as a global society, we are making progress toward this paradigm shift in many cultures.

Compare our grandmothers' situations in their societies to the positions our daughters have today:

- Women are much better educated now; and in some countries, the majority of students are female – the first time this has occurred since the 13th century.

- More women are in leadership positions now – in politics, public administration and business.

These developments indicate that we are starting to bring out more and more matrifocal values and that the paradigm shift towards a more balanced matrifocal/ patrifocal partnership has started. Great start – but much more is required to achieve true balance.

And Now, It's Your Turn

In this chapter, we described the enormous imbalance between matrifocal and patrifocal values almost everywhere in our world. This we must change to ensure sustainability of our societies, of humanity.

Now it's your turn. We challenge you to get up and move and lead through this paradigm shift. Go.

First, as a Woman

- Find the balance within yourself of your matrifocal and patrifocal values.
- Enforce and demand partnership of your matrifocal values with men's patrifocal focus.

Second, as a Man

- Bring out your own matrifocal values, balancing them with your patrifocal values within yourself.
- Recognize women, with their dominantly matrifocal values, as partners in their own right. Accept that they feel and decide things differently and that this "other way" of focusing on resilience adds significant value to both the sustainability of your partnerships and to our world.

Third, as Leaders

- Accept the responsibility to bring whatever you lead to a balance of matrifocal and patrifocal values.

That's the second paradigm shift Bernard Lietaer challenges you to go through and lead others through. Let us now tackle the third one: how and why we must go through a deep paradigm shift in how we use proprietary information.

6

Paradigm Shift 3: Towards More Personal Ownership of Information

This is true Liberty when free born men having to advise the public may speak free?

~ Euripides, Greek Philosopher, 484-406 B.C.

This paradigm shift concerns the human information system, the flow of information between humans that is vital for mankind. In this flow we generate, own and share information in our societies.

The Human Information System

Proprietary Information

We generate information as individuals, and it is our property. We decide - and nobody else does – what we consider our proprietary information: the photographs we took on our last trip to Paris, the books we wrote, but also our birth date, mailing address, credit card numbers, national identity numbers. Note that there is a difference between personal and proprietary or private information. Personal information is information about another person; private information is what we want to keep from public view.

Flow is Sharing of Proprietary Information

If we just compile information without sharing it with others, there is no flow of information; and the human information system comes to a standstill.

To share, we exchange proprietary information with our close friends. Another example would be sharing information among the team that finalized this book. So, we grant them – our social circle of proprietary information – access to some of our information.

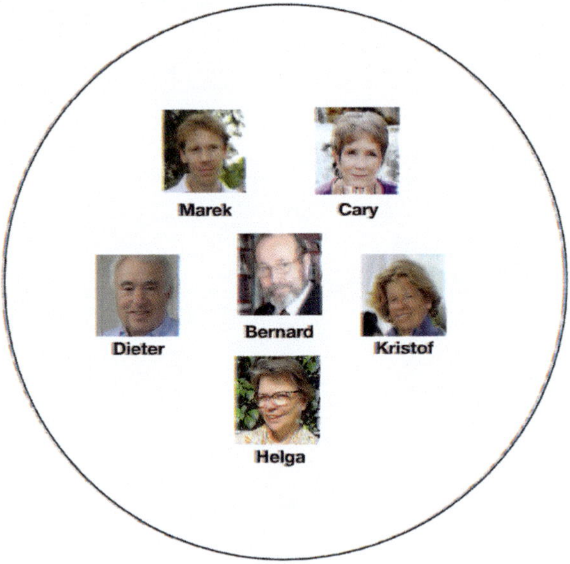

Fig. 17: Bernard Lietaer's circle of information for writing this book.

Sharing of information in flow, however, does not mean that we give up ownership of that information. If, for example, we grant our bank access to our mailing address, they may use this information – but they do not own it.

It is our own decision what we share, to whom we grant access, as well as the purposes for which they may use it.

Everyone Has Their Own Circles of Information

Every person has her or his own circles of information in which they make information flow by sharing and exchanging. Some of these circles may overlap: a person in our circle may also be a member of somebody else's circle of information.

Fig. 18: Everyone has their own circle of information.

In our illustration, Kristof's and Helga's circles, for instance, only overlap with Bernard's. Marek's circle, however, overlaps with Bernard's, Cary's and Dieter's.

Sharing, however, does not mean that we relinquish the ownership of our own proprietary information.

In the same sense, a group of people – like an institution – may own information. It could be a legal entity like a corporation, a professional association like a group of lawyers, a department within a larger corporation, etc. The principle is the same as for individuals: that group owns the information it creates and decides what to share and with whom.

Unconstrained Flow of Information Essential

Flow of information free of constraints is essential for living systems.

To underscore the importance of unconstrained flow of information in human societies, the Universal Declaration of Human Rights (UDHR) recognizes the importance of freedom to seek, receive and impart information as a human right under Article 19. Also, the same is acknowledged in international human rights law in the International Covenant on Civil and Political Rights (ICCPR).[34]

Decentralized Information Systems for Unconstrained Flow

In the 1980s at the European Organization for Nuclear Research (CERN), Tim Berners-Lee designed a method for sharing documents which was called the Internet and later evolved into what we know today as the World Wide Web. Its purpose was to "connect knowledge" – an unhindered flow of proprietary information. Commercial benefit was not its purpose.

The computer system supporting this setup was decentralized: no central computer was required to keep information flowing. All information was proprietary: kept and owned by individuals or groups.

[34] https://www.ohchr.org/en/professionalinterest/pages/ccpr.aspx

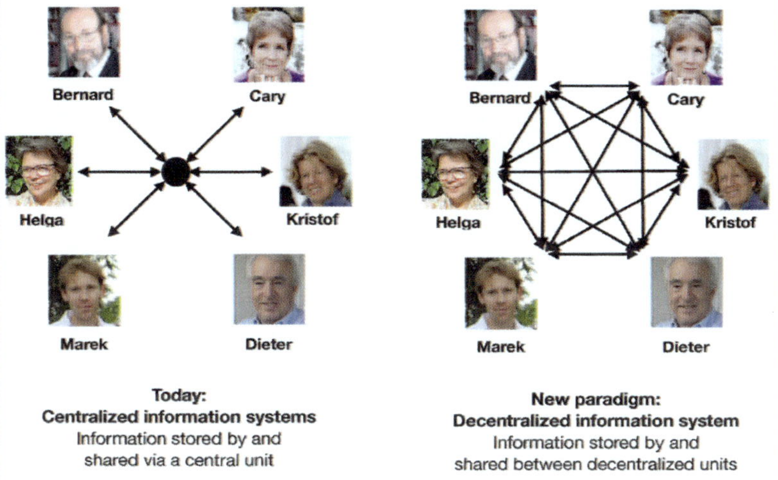

Fig. 19: From today's centralized to a decentralized paradigm for sustainability of the human information system.

Another term frequently used is "distributed information." We use this term to describe how information is stored in a computer network: If information is distributed, the same information resides with each user. If it is not, one or a few users have control of it. Both centralized and decentralized information systems can have information stored in distributed or non-distributed arrangements.

Centralized Information Systems: Proprietary Information, Filtered for Money

Then businesses found ways to make money from the human information system. For that purpose, the obvious design of the supporting information system was to centralize it. They took possession of people's proprietary information from their flow of information and centralized it in large data centers.

Not only that: To pass information between users as "search results," they filter out what they don't want us to receive and amplify what they want us to see. This happens on a large scale in our most frequently used communications tool, the Internet.

Vision and mission statements of such businesses disclose that intent:

- Providing access to the world's information, organizing it and making it universally accessible requires taking possession of proprietary information; and
- Usefulness of information is determined by the profit resulting from presenting it to users.

Vision

Provide access to the world's information

Mission:

1. Organize the world's information

2. Make it universally accessible

3. And useful

Fig. 20: Vision and mission of a centralized information system.

The most personal information about your online habits is collected, bought and sold, often instantaneously and invisibly. Data collection is a business driven by profits at consumers' expense.

~ Jackie Speier, American Politician

Constrains the Human Information System

By this process, the Web actually constrains sustainability of the human information system.

In our body, our nervous system manages the flow of information. A stroke or brain attack may, in the worst case, cut off the flow of information to large areas of our body.

In societies, the flow of information can be compared to the nervous system. By hindering or limiting (constraining) that flow, we reduce a society's ability to adjust, to learn, or in terms of the law of sustainability: we reduce our social system's resilience by reducing its diversity and interconnections.

Thus, hindering information flow in living systems causes them to become brittle, and in the worst case, crash.

The press was to serve the governed, not the governors.

~ U.S. Supreme Court Justice Hugo Black
in New York Times Co. v. United States (1971)

As Tim Berners-Lee said in an interview with *Vanity Fair*, July 1, 2018:[35]

> *We demonstrated that the Web had failed instead of served humanity, as it was supposed to have done, and failed in many places… The increasing centralization of the Web has ended up producing – with no deliberate action of the people who designed the platform – a large-scale emergent phenomenon which is anti-human.*

---

35 https://www.vanityfair.com/news/2018/07/the-man-who-created-the-world-wide-web-has-some-regrets

Exponentially More Invasive

An example is highlighted by the *New York Times'* Privacy Project. A recent posting outlines how digital advertisers use a variety of sources to aggregate a huge amount of data about individuals, using it for profit by enabling them to better target their ads and without any permission from consumers about the use of that information.[36] Aggregated information is not only acquired from the normal list and demographic sources, but is also accumulated from the kinds of posts an individual places on social media, online search history, purchase history and more. Frederike Kaltheuner, who heads the corporate exploitation program at Privacy International,[37] states "It's become exponentially more invasive, and most people are completely unaware of what kinds of data feeds into the targeting." If you have a home assistant product like Amazon's Alexa, private conversations may also be incorporated into this targeting effort without your knowledge.

Another recent blatant example: a private company working in the UK's National Health Service has been fined for selling more than 30m records of information about new mothers and their babies to data brokers and marketing firms.[38]

Who Cares?

Not only do we now lose ownership of our proprietary information to centralizing organizations, but strangely, many people don't even care about that loss of ownership – even if they are aware that if they are not paying for something, they are not the customer, but the product being sold.

---

36 https://www.nytimes.com/interactive/2019/04/30/opinion/privacy-targeted-advertising.html

37 https://privacyinternational.org

38 https://www.ft.com/content/6954971e-5d3a-11e9-939a-341f5ada9d40?mc_cid=e16fae871c&mc_eid=4e204fdf93

We might suspect that such expropriation and centralization of proprietary information is treated like a fait accompli – you know about it, but you feel helplessly exposed, see no alternative, and therefore, just don't mention it or take any action to correct it.

The Paradigm Shift Required: Towards More Personal Ownership of Proprietary Information

According to the law of sustainability, dispossessing and centralizing positions our human information system in the efficiency corner, making our society increasingly vulnerable to instability and political crisis.

We need a significant paradigm shift to recover from this dramatic change in the use of information by third parties. Awareness of this necessity is growing – but we need to reverse this trend to avoid paying a high price for the consequences of continuing in the wrong direction.

Information Technology and Governments Must Join Forces

Moving from the present centralization of information systems to a decentralized setup will be a major paradigm shift. Two domains must join forces to bring this shift about.

Information technology must bring information systems to a truly decentralized setup, ceding ownership of all proprietary information to the individual user. Governments must support information technology's move with adequate legislation.

In other words, that means that information technology must provide a truly decentralized "my digital self" identity with the ability for all people to define their own proprietary information and to decide with whom they want to share it.

Information Technology Already on the Move

As of today, in information technology everyone talks about decentralization. Not only do people demand ownership of their proprietary information and unfiltered flow of public information, but with the Internet of Things around the corner people are also recognizing the immense inherent risk of centralized information systems. As a worst case example, a business owning centralized information about self-driving cars would have the power to turn off these cars anywhere in the world.

Edge computing, which brings computer data storage closer to the location where it is needed, is sometimes positioned as step toward decentralization. However, from the point of view of the law of sustainability, this technology aims at increasing the efficiency of central ownership of information – not at increasing personal ownership of private information.

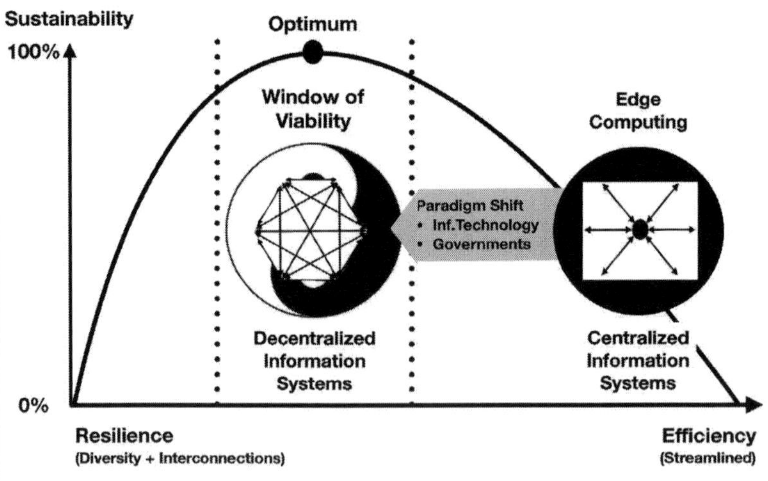

Fig. 21: For sustainability of the human information system, information technology and governments must join forces.

Blockchain – an important and very reliable invention – shows promise as a way to deliver full distribution of information and is an important step in the direction of achieving this paradigm shift. It opens new ways of reaching consensus and has the potential for decentralization, but presently is not used for that purpose. Further development is required to design Blockchain for the purpose of truly decentralized management of information.

Innovators Taking the Lead

Some innovators are already taking the lead in the paradigm shift toward fully decentralized circular information systems. Examples include:

One example is SOLID, a new project led by Tim Berners-Lee, taking place at the Massachusetts Institute of Technology (MIT). The project aims to radically change the way Web applications work today, resulting in true ownership of proprietary information.

THREEFOLD is another technology development in that direction. They also offer tools for true delivery of decentralized information management.

There are several other active initiatives that aim at allowing individuals to share their personal information within their self-defined circles, with real and full decentralization.

Governments Must Provide Laws to Strengthen Private Ownership of Information

Information technology companies cannot deliver this paradigm shift on their own. Governments must support them with legislation enabling personal ownership of information.

As always when mankind goes through a turning point into a new paradigm, legislators struggle. Often they are late to recognize that the new paradigm requires revision of present laws or even new laws. Lawmakers are typically stuck in the previous paradigm and struggle to foresee the consequences of the new laws they design. An example from Switzerland:[39] the Canton of Grison in 1900 forbid the use of cars (new paradigm) on its roads based on the reasoning that they make horses shy and are dangerous for other traffic (previous paradigm). It took till June 21, 1925, to change that law and allow cars to be used. Human history is filled with similar cases, as Barbara W. Tuchman writes in her famous book *The March of Folly.*

The human information system is no exception. It reacts to attempts (laws) to change it not directly, but in loops (see chapter on Aristotle's logic). It therefore easily happens that well-meant legislation results in unforeseen negative constraints, reducing instead of increasing sustainability. Especially if legislators are still stuck in the previous paradigm they struggle to design helpful laws for the new paradigm.

In the European Union (EU), for example, new copyright laws were approved by the EU parliament with the goal of protecting and respecting proprietary information. Some IT experts, however, observe[40] that these well-meant laws result in seriously constraining the human information system as noted in an article headlined: "the European Union prepares to wreck internet with new copyright law."

They especially point out[41] that Article 11 (reproducing more than "single words or very short extracts" of news stories will require a license – also from individuals), and

---

39 https://www.nzz.ch/schweiz/schweizer-geschichte/sonderfall-graubuenden-der-kampf-ums-automobil-ld.103634

40 https://www.zdnet.com/article/the-eus-new-copyright-laws-threaten-to-destroy-the-internet

41 https://juliareda.eu/2019/02/eu-copyright-final-text

Article 13 (requiring web sites to preemptively buy licenses for anything that users may possibly upload) will result in handing over the Internet to the few biggest players like Google, Amazon, etc., and lock out small businesses or individual users from the flow of human information.

As we said before: we consider this a typical development in a paradigm shifting turning point and expect legislators (also the EU) to ultimately adjust their laws to better focus on and enable the goal of the sustainability of the human information system.

An example in that regard is the Contract for the Web, which was "designed as a mechanism for each party to be held accountable for doing their part to build an open and free web," and lays out Contract Principles for governments, companies and citizens.

And Now, It's Your Turn

On the previous pages, we shared how ownership of our proprietary information has been taken away from us with the intention to make money from it.

Now, centralized organizations determine which information we receive – in other words, how we perceive our world and its future. In effect, they constrain the human information system and act as censors. This has been clearly demonstrated by how some governments have been able to use personal information to destabilize competing governments, interfere in their elections, and sow social discord by creating "bubbles" in which consumers are provided with information, factual or not, that is designed to help radicalize their beliefs.

The law of sustainability states that this type of development blocks our ability to achieve and maintain the sustainability of our world.

All dictatorships in human history have had a censorship policy with the key goal of determining what people should know, read or say. George Orwell's book *1984* described a society where the "ministry of truth" determined what the citizens read or saw on TV. With a development like Orwell described, we would not be able to keep the world sustainable. In fact, on the 70th anniversary of Orwell's book, there has been a great deal of discussion in the media comparing the current state in some countries of the world with the "ministry of truth" situation Orwell described.

Paradigm 3 is primarily about how we use private information and how information technology enables that. Therefore, our call to action goes to all our leaders and decision makers – in politics, business and anywhere else.

First, as Leaders in Politics, Business or Anywhere Else

- Set Priority Number 1 to sustainability of our world.
- To do so, lead the re-establishment of personal ownership of proprietary information in your areas of responsibility, counteracting the trend towards centralization and keeping centralization to the absolute minimum necessary.

Second, as Experts, Wherever You Work

- In whatever you design – especially for the coming world of IoT (Internet of Things): put sustainability of our human information system first, and
- Contribute to it by enabling personal ownership of proprietary information.

Third, as an Individual

- Defend your right of personal ownership of your proprietary information day by day,

- Give preference to organizations and leaders who enable that ownership and
- Resist any trend to expropriate your proprietary information.

What Bernard Promised and What This Book Delivered

In his letter to you at the beginning of this book, dear reader, Bernard promised to make you aware of three paradigm shifts that are essential to changing our world for the better:

1. To go through a paradigm shift in perception, from Aristotle's linear logic to the Tao view: to accept and deeply understand the law of sustainability and how it applies to individual living systems as well as to our entire world.
2. To go through a paradigm shift in cultural values: understanding how we are out of balance between patrifocal and matrifocal values and how we must bring this imbalance back into balance.
3. To go through a paradigm shift with respect to information: how we tumbled out of balance, had ownership of our private information taken away – and how we can take it back, with the help of our governments and information technology companies and professionals.

Again, with this book Bernard challenges you to personally go through these paradigm shifts yourself, to demand these shifts wherever you live and work, and to lead them, if you have a leadership position – whether as President of a country, an international organization or as responsible member of a small community.

Yours is the world of tomorrow. Go ahead and create it!

If world problems feel too big to tackle, think small.
Step by step. Small wins build confidence,
lead the way to change.

~ Rosabeth Moss Kanter, Author of
"The Change Masters"

For more information about Bernard Lietaer and achieving the paradigm shifts described in this book, and to join the global conversation, please visit https://sustainable-world.ch.

Four Books, One Article

Over Bernard's long career, he has written a large number of books on monetary and financial topics. This book refers to four of them and one paper, which he sees as especially important for the paradigm shifts discussed here. We recommend reading them if you wish to delve further into the topics addressed in this book.

Mysterium Geld

Publisher: Epubli, Germany.

ISBN: 200-0-040182-8-25 (English version in preparation)

In this book, Bernard describes a society's collective emotions and how they form its monetary system. In the last 500 years, the archetype of the Great Mother – symbol of nature, fertility and abundance – was systematically suppressed – leading to dominantly patrifocal values at the expense of matrifocal values.

Money and Sustainability

A report from the Club of Rome – EU Chapter

Publisher: Triarchy Press, 2012. ISBN: 978-1-908009-7-53

In this book (written with Christian Arnsperger, Sally Goerner and Stefan Brunnhuber), Bernard discusses in detail the position of our traditional money in the law of sustainability. We consider it as essential reading for policymakers, business leaders and economists, anyone concerned with sustainability, those working in the field of monetary systems and anyone with an informed interest in the future of our planet.

Creating Wealth – Growing Local Economies with Local Currencies

Gwendolyn Hallsmith & Bernard Lietaer

Publisher: New Society Publishers, 2011.

ISBN: 978-0-86571-667-4

This book – based on a large number of projects for complementary currencies – describes in detail the reasons for implementing them, the projects you need launch and drive through and critical factors for success.

Rethinking Money – How New Currencies Turn Scarcity Into Prosperity

With Jacqui Dunne

Publisher: Berret-Koehler, 2013. ISBN: 978-1-60994-296-0

In this book, Jacqui and Bernard give an updated view of our traditional monetary system and offer strategies for dual monetary systems for banking, business and entrepreneurs, governments and NGOs.

"A World in Balance"

(PDF, available for download)

https://www.academia.edu/15398979/A_World_in_Balance

In this article Bernard discusses in more detail patrifocal and matrifocal values and how they drive a society's monetary system, and especially describe a flourishing dual currency system in Bali.

About Bernard Lietaer[42]

Bernard Lietaer (February 7, 1942 – February 4, 2019) was a civil engineer, economist, author and professor.

He studied engineering at the University of Leuven, where he went back as a professor of international finance from 1975-1978 and again from 1983-1986.

When he went to MIT in the U.S., he started working as well for McCormick Consultants. Because of his post-graduate thesis, "Financial management of Foreign Exchange. An Operational Technique to Reduce Risk," in 1969, he was chosen by *Time Magazine* as one of the ten best business students in America that year. When it was published as a book in 1971, just after President Nixon took the dollar off the gold standard, it turned out to be the only systematic research which could be used with all of the major currencies of the world.

Continuing to work on this subject, he discovered the link between our monetary system and misery; and in 1978, he published the book *A Role for Europe in the North-South Conflict.*

---

[42] https://www.revolvy.com/page/Bernard-Lietaer

During his time at the Central Bank in Belgium (National Bank of Belgium), he was the president of Belgium's Electronic Payment System and implemented the convergence mechanism (ECU) to the single European currency system.

He co-founded one of the largest and most successful currency management firms, Gaia Corp, and managed an offshore currency fund (Gaia Hedge II) which was the world's top performing managed currency fund during the 1987-91 period while he ran it. *Business Week* named him "the world's top currency trader" in 1992.

In 1991, he obtained the book *Interest and Inflation Free Money* written by Margrit Kennedy (German version published in 1990), which made him finally understand the most important problems of our monetary system. He started fundamental research about the subject of money, which resulted in two books: *The Future of Money*, 1999, and *Mysterium Geld* (Mystery of Money), 2000.

As a consequence, he developed the idea of Complementary Currencies, which he spread in several books, also together with Margrit Kennedy and other authors as well as in other publications, numerous conferences, as a professor at different universities and a consultant tot companies, organizations and governments worldwide.

In 2009 he found – with Robert E. Ulanowicz and Sally J. Goerner, based on the research of Ulanowicz – the Law of Sustainability, the scientific proof that as monocultures, our actual monetary systems are very unstable over the long term. In the publication *Money and Sustainability – The Missing Link* of the Club of Rome, he pointed out, with Christian Arnsperger, Sally J. Goerner and Stefan Brunnhuber, that our monetary system drives our world out of sustainability.

Epilogue

Two important endorsements for this book are better read after the reader has absorbed the context of this book. We thank both Marc Dubrulle and Father Simon Pierre for their thoughtful contributions to this book.

Marc Dubrulle

Ex officio Member of the Club of Rome, President emeritus, The Club of Rome EU-Chapter

The Superb Legacy of a Visionary Monetarist

Bernard Lietaer saw far and deep. Perhaps too far and too deep. His thinking was audacious and bold. Questioning the mainstream assumptions from monetarists, financiers, bankers, economists and political leaders is disruptive. Moving on these grounds leads to dismissal or – worse – to ignorance and indifference.

I made Bernard's acquaintance more than ten years ago in the Club of Rome (CoR) EU-Chapter. We were both Board members. When elected President, I started looking with more detail into his career, expertise and publications. We had most pleasant and stimulating conversations, often over a friendly private lunch or with a glass of Belgian Trappist beer after a meeting.

Sustainability was at the core of the Club's concerns, but little attention had been paid to monetary issues. They were thought too highly technical, requiring solid financial expertise. However, at our Aurelio Peccei Lectures & Dialogues on 19 February 2009, Bernard was invited to present his views on systemic solutions for today's world challenges. They obviously referred to money systems. We both felt there was room for a specific analysis of these systems and their possible alternatives. The first drafts of a manuscript were already available, with contributions from Christian Arnsperger, Sally Goerner and Stefan Brunnhuber.

In 2011, Finance Watch was founded as a European NGO in reaction to the last financial crisis, when policymakers realised that there was no counter-power to the finance lobby. Its first Secretary General, Thierry Philipponat, was invited with me for a lunch at Bernard's flat. We discussed the project of a report from the CoR-EU to Finance Watch. The idea was to expose the systemic flaws in our money system and the wrong thinking underpinning it, leading to the financial catastrophes. The report would set out practical proposals for creating a money 'ecosystem' with complementary currencies to support and stabilise the current money system.

Thierry Philipponat was enthused. The link between money and sustainability was established. Dennis Meadows, co-author of Limits to Growth, agreed to write a foreword which is very enlightening: …*We will never create sustainability while immersed in the present financial system. I used not to think this. Indeed, I did not think about the money system at all. I took it for granted as a neutral and inevitable aspect of human society. But… now I understand, as proven clearly in this text, that the prevailing financial system is incompatible with sustainability.*

It is the undeniable merit of Bernard Lietaer to have revealed this crucial issue for all those who endeavour to make the planet and quality of life sustainable. The report *Money and Sustainability: The Missing Link*, was published in

2012 by Triarchy Press, UK, endorsed by the Board of the CoR-EU, presented to Finance Watch and the World Business Academy with a launch event at the University Foundation in Brussels on 30 May 2012.

Bernard's world view obviously reached far beyond monetary affairs, his professional expertise. He had this holistic approach which is too often missing when addressing the many problems of today's civilisation. He was a humanist in the most positive sense of the word, caring for more equity and justice. Above all he had a strong willpower, looking at the future with optimism. His latest book is a superb legacy to all of us and a challenge to review our obsolete models.

Father Simon Pierre

Father Simon Pierre is, perhaps, Bernard's oldest friend. He is a Benedictine Monk from the monastery of Wavreumont Belgium, living in the monastic foundation in Perú since 1974 and more specifically, since 1992, in the midst of the indigenous Aymara people near Titicaca lake.

In Loving Tribute to Bernard Lietaer, My Friend

In Bernard's long list of friends, I must probably be one of the first, since we met in adolescence: I was 14, he must have been 18 or 19. We were, on the surface, at the opposite end of the spectrum: I wanted to become a Benedictine monk, which I ultimately did become, and he was already searching all over for the meaning of reality, visible and hidden, and how to approach it with intelligence and heart. Since then, however, our friendship has been forged through an uninterrupted Yin-Yang conversation between mysticism and utopia, a mysterious and silent contrivance that only death seemed to be able to suspend at its peak.

I would like to thank the authors of this book for allowing me to resume the conversation beyond the mystery of the invisible. They encourage me to resume, on the basis of the three paradigm shifts proposed here, an ever-open debate between the monk and the visionary, both researchers, on different paths, of the "indispensable impossible" that we call hope.

But I am not here to talk about "him and me," which belongs only to him and to me, but to reread with you the invitation of this book from where I am in my human and spiritual adventure. I will therefore allow myself to react to the paradigms proposed here from two points of view: culture and mysticism.

Culture as a transversal axis

As every time we open a debate, I will allow myself to propose once again a fundamental objection to Bernard's hypotheses, not to deny their relevance, but to broaden their horizons.

Is the efficiency-resilience binomial not too narrow and will we not run the risk of consolidating, by making it more flexible, the system of Western civilization, which, obviously, dehumanizes the world in many respects? I have always admired, of course, the West's ability to adapt and correct itself so as not to fundamentally question its own dogmas of progress. No culture and no system have, like us, the ability to constantly recreate itself and never really question itself.

Is this not still the risk of this paradigm shift: reinventing in order not to change? Who, indeed, would not agree with Bernard's beautiful utopia? The future of the planet, but above all the continuity of the Western world view, depends on it. But is that the priority?

The missing link of cultures

Having myself lived in the heart of the indigenous cultures of the Peruvian Andes for many years, I have learned to radically challenge my European dogmas about happiness, life and the world. There are really other ways of looking at man and in particular the relationship of differences between humans and the whole cosmos.

The first revolution is anthropological. Is the human being, conceived as an individual, really the center of the world? Is the West's exacerbated anthropocentrism good news for the world? In the traditional cultures of the Andes (and this is probably not the only case), the community exists before the individual; and the human being recognizes himself only in the relationship of reciprocity.

Thus, the patrifocal paradigm and the matrifocal paradigm are not two complementary points of view, but a unique movement of reciprocity. We can even go further and wonder, with these traditional cultures, if humans have a privileged function compared to the rest of the inhabitants of the universe. In non-Western cultures, very often harmony, preserved and constantly restored among all living beings, is the true goal of life in and the universe, not sustainability first and foremost. Efficiency and resilience are absolutely absent from this intuition.

This diversity of cosmovision, implicit anthropologies and utopias is always present in the collective unconscious. A people may well superficially adopt the categories of Western rationality; and even if corrected and softened, its deep being always continues to react and feel in tune with its roots.

It therefore seems essential to me to submit the new paradigms we are talking about here to the judgment and transformative melting pot of cultures in their specificity. It is certainly unthinkable today to exclude Western rationality, which has become the heritage of all humanity. But it can, and must, be rethought from top to bottom, based on other, healthier and more humane approaches. Universal violence, generated by the imposition of Western categories on the world, certainly has its origin, for the most part, in the forgetting of the wisdom embodied in the cultures of yesterday and today.

The symbolic dimension

An increasingly absent dimension of Western rationality has much to do with symbolism and poetics. We have separated these spaces to such an extent that they no longer have any real interconnection. Everyone moves in their own universe.

In non-Western cultures, symbolism and poetics are intimately integrated. We are even talking about symbolic technology and the intrinsic rituality of human action. It is precisely in this field, symbolic and ritual, that the human community not only reappropriates all the information, as implied by the third shift of paradigms, but also reinterprets and re-enchants it, in some way.

Without this re-enchantment of the world, in the multiplicity of peoples' intuitions, the new paradigms will never be anything more than a change of clothes that are more flexible, more adapted but just as foreign to the body that wears them.

The ethical dimension

Even if resilience corrects blind efficiency, and patri- and matri-focal dynamics humanize in diversity, just as the reappropriation of information allows critical discernment and decision making, it cannot be denied that recent developments in the West have largely removed the notion of ethics from decisions and choices.

Certainly, democratic humanism imposes a series of normative conditions and limits on the blind voracity of the market. But this is hardly the case in the vast majority of countries in the world, including the United States. The universal economic dogma of profit seems infallible and above the ethical requirements of States and multinational communities.

Introduce mysticism into decisions?

It seems very insulting, even absurd, to speak of mysticism in this context. And yet, the unpredictable whims of reality, even the market, seem to tell us that there is a dimension of mystery in the world that must be taken into account and that has to do with the unpredictability of the human being. Is there not a massive form of arrogance in the very notion of sustainability, as if we could finally foresee and manage everything?

As monks, we claim to be witnesses of this mystery, of this unpredictability of reality, of the beyond of all our achievements in the invisible. Madness necessary for a world that breathes beyond its forecasts and readjustments, even brilliant ones.

Ethics as a prerequisite

I mentioned above the absence of ethical criteria in most of our political and economic decisions. Eventually we ask ourselves the question *a posteriori.* Ethics, as a consequence of mysticism, is, on the contrary, a necessary *a priori*, a condition for any decision and any discernment.

For a long time, I have advocated the creation of an ethical United Nations, where all the world's wisdoms would share their spiritual and ethical foundations, to manage the political, economic and social world. This was the meaning, I believe, of President Mitterrand's creation of his famous multi-philosophical ethics committee. But it seems to have been a long time coming.

The dialogue has resumed

These are some of the follies of an atypical monk, who looks at his friend Bernard's utopias, as we have always done, from the friend's heart, but with the distance that any true friendship always allows.

I can already hear his silent response from the absolute mystery where he now lives, and I await this reply with impatience and joy. But it will be done in another space.

Forgive me for this shared nonsense. But I know that Bernard was essentially a mystic and that he has known, since our beginnings in adolescence, this particular song scratched on a mysterious guitar of silence.

Thank you, Bernard.

Index

D

E

F

G

H

I

K

L

M

N

O

P

R

W

Y

Z